Healthy JUNK

by **SHARNY & JULIUS**

healthy versions of
your favourite junk foods!

www.sharnyandjulius.com
email:sharnyandjulius@
sharnyandjulius.com

Cover Photography: sharnyandjulius

Typesetting and Design: sharnyandjulius

ISBN: 978-0-9923613-0-3

HEALTHY JUNK

HEALTHY VERSIONS OF YOUR FAVOURITE JUNK FOODS!

OVER 50 DELICIOUS RECIPES

sugar free
wheat free
grain free
nut free
dairy free
additive free
preservative free
guilt free
paleo friendly

ohhh so tasty!

SHARNY ♾ JULIUS
www.sharnyandjulius.com

Other titles by **SHARNY & JULIUS**

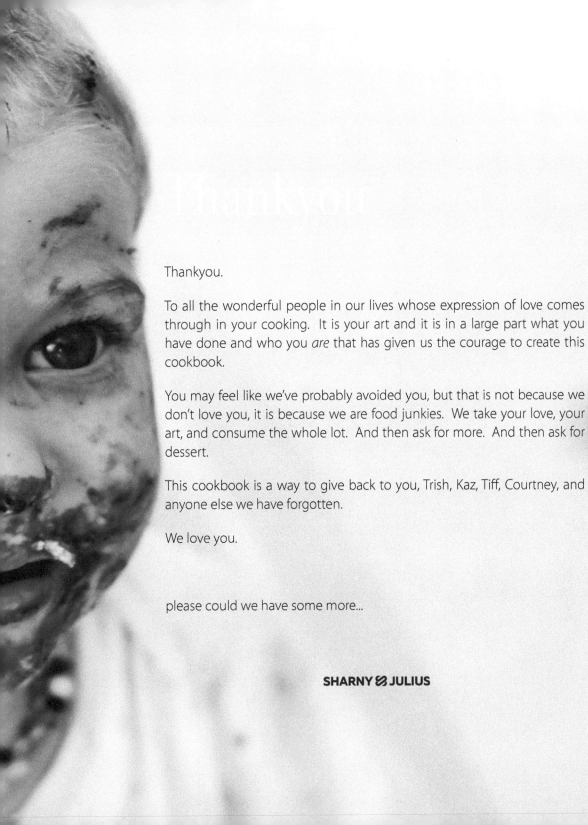

Thankyou.

To all the wonderful people in our lives whose expression of love comes through in your cooking. It is your art and it is in a large part what you have done and who you *are* that has given us the courage to create this cookbook.

You may feel like we've probably avoided you, but that is not because we don't love you, it is because we are food junkies. We take your love, your art, and consume the whole lot. And then ask for more. And then ask for dessert.

This cookbook is a way to give back to you, Trish, Kaz, Tiff, Courtney, and anyone else we have forgotten.

We love you.

please could we have some more...

SHARNY ⊘ JULIUS

Why this book is so important to us!

It's no secret that we are food addicts. Well, let's be a bit more accurate, we are not addicted to food - we are addicted to junk food. Burgers, pizza, fries, chips, wedges, sauces, chocolate. All the stuff that we shouldn't have, we can't stop thinking about (or, once we get a little taste, can't stop eating until it is all gone!)

Finally becoming clean in our eating was one of the hardest things we've ever done in our lives. And it's the same for anybody else we have spoken to. Giving up our favourite foods was the worst part. "I'm never going to eat pizza again" is a hard thing to say. "Chocolate..." we said with longing; Willy Wonka laughing manically in the background...

We couldn't do it. We've been back too many times and that is why we created this cookbook. It is because broccoli and chicken breasts are just not enough for us. We grew up in food families where love was shared around the dinner table, where footy was watched in front of the TV with a big bowl of chips. Where cookies were waiting at Nannas house, for hungry little mouths.

For us to become healthy, we had to stop visiting friends all together, and it's near impossible to go our for dinner to a nice restaurant and just order a salad without getting a "you're one of those" stares and a large bill for what is essentially just lettuce.

So we started experimenting at home.

Could we make our favourite foods, without all the junk in them? No sugar, no wheat (no grains), no dairy, no additives (aritificial colours, sweeteners, preservatives) and no nuts (Julius is allergic to nuts, they are certainly not junk).

Yes we bloody well can, and SO CAN YOU!!

This book is a culmination of 60 of our favourite recipes. It's a way of us saying "please invite us back for dinner," and for our kids it is a way for them to experience the kind of love only food can give, love that just doesn't come from chicken breast and broccoli. A love that for them, will now come guilt free.

Enjoy sharing and creating these meals with your family, and please let us know what you think on our website: sharnyandjulius.com

Menu

(in alphabetical order, because when it comes to junk food, well, there is no 'right time'...)

Baking Powder

Ingredients:

1 cup bicarbonate soda

2 cups cream of tartar

1 tsp arrowroot powder

(To be extra healthy, make sure your ingredients are organic and check the label to make sure nothing else is added)

We make our own baking powder so we know what is in it.

Being such an integral part of so many baking recipes, we think it's best if you know what's in yours too. You could just buy it if you like, but it's just as easy to make up a big batch once and forget it.

How to make:

Mix the bicarb soda and cream of tartar together until well combined.

Use immediately.

To store baking powder:

Add a teaspoon of arrowroot to the mixture, and stir. This will absorb any moisture from the air, and prevent the baking powder from reacting before you need it. Store in an air-tight container.

Did you know?

Most commercial baking powder contains aluminium to prevent reacting with the moisture in the air, so make your own and avoid all that aluminium, in case you become like wolverine.

Banana Bread

Ingredients:

2 large ripe bananas

¼ cup sunflower or coconut oil

1 tbsp baking powder

3 eggs

½ cup banana flour

¼ cup of coconut nectar (optional)

There is nothing more delicious than a winter banana bread, fresh out of the oven. Unfortunately, it has been out of bounds for most health conscious individuals.

Until now...

How to make:

Preheat oven to 180°C.

In a large bowl or blender, mix the ingredients until smooth and fluffy.

Pour the mixture into a small, non-stick bread tin.

Bake for 30 - 45 minutes.

Allow to cool before removing from tray.

Barbeque Sauce

Ingredients:

1 cup of tomato sauce (see our recipe on page 120)

½ cup water

1 medium onion

½ cup apple cider vinegar

2 tbsp molasses

1 tbsp Worcestershire sauce

¼ tsp all-spice mix

¼ tsp Himalayan sea salt

¼ tsp cinnamon

Ooh baby. Back when we were kids, adults used to call barbeque sauce the food killer, because it took away the flavour of everything and replaced it with the sweet, yet tangy and smoky magic delight we all know as barbeque sauce.

The more we were told we weren't allowed it, the more we had it. So here it is, in all it's miraculous glory - a healthy barbeque sauce.

How to make:

Add all the ingredients to a saucepan and stir to combine.

Make it boil like a witches broth.

Reduce heat so it can simmer uncovered for about 15 minutes.

Simmer longer if you like it thicker.

Makes about 1 ½ cups of food killer.

Did you know?

Molasses is what's left over after the sugar is extracted from the sugarcane plant.

Blueberry Muffins

Ingredients:

½ cup coconut flour

¼ cup banana flour

1 tbsp baking powder

4 eggs

2 tbsp coconut oil

1 tsp ground cinnamon

1 large mango flesh mashed like puree

200g fresh or frozen blueberries

*NOTE: You can use any fruit combinations you like, we just love the mango and blueberry combo!

Most coffee shops have a stack of fresh blueberry muffins sitting there on the shelf, sweet aroma drifting into your nostrils with a feeling of love. Tummy love.

Before you know it, you're half way through your second one and about $10 short on pocket money. NO MORE!

Make your own blueberry muffins out of healthy ingredients and boggle your friends! While you're getting shredded eating "junk", they're ordering skinny long blacks because "they're watching their calories..."

How to make:

Preheat the oven to 180°C.

Combine all ingredients in a large bowl or blender (except blueberries).

Stir through the blueberries last.

Divide the mixture into non-stick muffin cups.

Bake for 30 – 45 minutes until cooked through and golden.

Did you know?

Blueberries are one of the lowest GI fruits you can get? Many 'diets' that say no to all fruit, allow you to have blueberries. They're like a loophole of deliciousness.

16

Bread

Ingredients:

¼ cup coconut flour

1 cup golden flaxmeal

Pinch of Himalayan sea salt

1 tbsp baking powder

3 eggs

2 tbsp coconut oil

¾ cup of water

¼ cup of sweetener like coconut nectar for sweet flavoured bread (optional)

Add some seeds to make it look more expensive. Just like a bakery. (optional)

Bread is one of those staples that is hard to get over. The first time some health guru nutcase told you that bread was making you fat was like telling you that you were no longer able to eat.

But as of now, you don't even have to give it up! In fact, eat even more bread, because it is healthy. If you have a relative who swears that seedy bread is so much classier, then throw in some seeds to make it look like the loaf on the left there.

P.S. this may be a heavier bread than you're used to, if you want it more moist, add water (1/2 cup at a time)

How to make:

Preheat oven to 180°C (350°F).

Mix all ingredients in a large bowl or blender.

Put the mixture to a small non-stick bread tin.

Bake for 30 - 45 minutes.

Let it cool for 10 minutes.

Add spread you favour like almond butter or avocado.

Brownies

Chocolate mixture:

3 tbsp coconut cream

¼ cup raw cacao powder

3 tbsp coconut oil

The rest:

½ cup coconut flour sifted

¼ tbsp baking powder

1 tsp Himalayan sea salt

½ cup coconut nectar

4 tbsp coconut oil

2 eggs whisked

¼ cup cooked and mashed pumpkin

This is possibly our favourite recipe in the whole book.

Soft, perfectly crumbly interior with just enough smooth crust on top to make your mouth fall in love.

Just make these, you'll love them too - they taste even better than their pants shrinking cousins.

How to make the chocolate mixture:

Melt coconut cream, cacao and 3 tablespoons coconut oil in a small saucepan over low heat.

How to make the rest:

Preheat oven to 180°C.

In a bowl, combine coconut flour, baking powder and salt.

Add the melted chocolate mixture, the coconut nectar, 4 more tablespoons of coconut oil, eggs and pumpkin to the dry ingredients.

Mix well.

Bake in a greased baking tray for 45 minutes.

Cool and slice.

Burger

When we were putting together the recipes in this book, we both agreed that if we could make a burger that looked like a burger and tasted just like a fast food burger, we would have the perfect cookbook.

We ended up making this bad boy on the right. It makes us salivate just looking at it; and the best part? It tastes even better than a real one. Much better.

Ingredients:

2 cups raw cauliflower

1 tbsp coconut flour

2 eggs

1 tsp garlic powder

½ tsp Himalayan sea salt

Dash of black pepper

½ tbsp sesame seeds

How to make:

Preheat the oven to 200°C.

Lightly cook cauliflower for a few minutes so it is soft but not falling apart.

Blend the cauliflower in a food processor.

Put the cauliflower in a small kitchen towel or a clean cloth and squeeze all the liquid out.

Put it on a large bowl and mix the rest of the ingredients together (except the sesame seeds).

Place the buns on a baking paper and shape them with your hands (you'll have to make the buns in halves like the picture on the left).

Sprinkle sesame seeds on top of the top-half.

Bake them in the oven for about 15 minutes.

Build your burger just like you would a normal one - pattie, lettuce, tomato, and all your favourite sauces.

Tomato sauce: page 120
Barbecue sauce: page 14
Mayonnaise: page 82

Cherry Ripe

A serving of our chocolate (see our recipe on page 28) before it is cooled in the fridge

½ cup goji berries

½ cup shredded coconut

Sharny's favourite chocolate bar. By far.

How to make:

Make up the chocolate in the same way as usual (page 28).

Pour half of the chocolate into a shallow dish.

Cover the chocolate with goji berries and coconut.

Pour over the remaining chocolate.

Cool in fridge.

Remove from dish and slice accordingly.

Chicken Strips

Ingredients:

2 boneless, skinless chicken breasts cut into strips

¼ cup coconut flour

¼ cup unsweetened shredded coconut

⅛ tsp Himalayan sea salt

1 egg

2 tbsp coconut oil

Fast food places came out a few years ago saying that they had created a healthy snack; the chicken strip (or chicken tender).

Plenty of overweight people became obese following that marketing disguised as advice.

Take back your waist without losing taste - here is a delicious chicken strip recipe... go on, you can go back for seconds.

How to make:

Mix coconut flour, shredded coconut and sea salt together in a bowl.

Beat egg in a separate bowl.

Dip chicken breast in egg, then roll in dry mixture.

Heat a frying pan over medium heat and add coconut oil when hot.

Pan fry until chicken is cooked through.

26

Chocolate

Seriously, chocolate. It tastes exactly the same, it has the same gentle, fine crumble that chocolate has, but we've managed to make it without sugar, without milk and without guilt.

And it's easier to make than sneaking one into the trolley without the checkout boy looking at your stomach!

Ingredients:

70g finely grated cacao butter

½ cup raw cacao powder, sifted*

2 tbsp coconut nectar

Pinch of Himalayan sea salt

Seeds from 2 vanilla pods

*If you prefer milkier chocolate (not so dark tasting), decrease the amount of raw cacao powder used.

How to make:

Melt cacao butter in a small, dry metal or glass bowl over a saucepan of simmering water.

Once melted, remove from heat and whisk in cacao powder, coconut nectar, salt and vanilla seeds.

Fill the chocolate moulds with mixture.

Refrigerate until set.

Hide it from the rest of the family (you'll want it all). But you don't need to hide yourself while you eat it anymore. This chocolate can be eaten outside of the pantry cupboard.

Did you know?

Cacao is one of nature's greatest antioxidants... so you better eat another piece.

Chocolate Bread

Why stop at white bread, when you can spit in the face of unhealthiness and make a chocolate bread complete with chocolate icing? And if you're really crazy, put some chocolate spread on it.

Then eat it all at a dietetics conference, you bad ass.

Ingredients:

½ cup banana flour

2 tbsp baking powder

1 pinch of Himalayan sea salt

¼ cup raw cacao powder

1 avocado, mashed

¼ cup coconut oil

¼ - ½ cup coconut nectar (depending on how sweet you want it)

2 eggs

How to make:

Preheat oven to 180°C.

Mix all ingredients in a large bowl or blender.

Pour the mixture into a small non-stick bread tin that is lined with baking paper.

Bake for 30 - 45 minutes.

Chocolate Cake

Cake Ingredients:

¼ cup cacao powder

¼ cup banana flour

¼ cup coconut flour

½ an avocado

1 tbsp baking powder

Pinch of Himalayan sea salt

3 eggs

½ cup coconut nectar

¼ cup melted coconut oil

½ cup water

Icing Ingredients:

3 tbsp coconut nectar

2 tbsp raw cacao powder

1 tbsp coconut oil

Is this the first recipe you turned to? It should be, it's freakin' delicious!

That cake right there looks like one you get from a coffee shop, complete with the last week's gossip and a large cappuccino, right?

Well, save yourself the gossip and the muffin top, cause you can now have your cake and eat it too!

How to make:

Preheat oven to 180°C.

Mix all ingredients together in a large bowl (blender is best).

Spoon the mixture into a cake tin, greased with coconut oil.

Bake for about 30 - 45 minutes.

Remove from the oven and allow to cool.

How to make the icing:

Stir all ingredients together.

Spread on your cake.

Chocolate Chip Cookies

Ingredients:

½ cup coconut flour

¼ cup flax meal

1 tbsp baking powder

¼ cup coconut oil

¼ cup coconut nectar

2 large eggs

¼ tsp Himalayan sea salt

½ cup chocolate chunks (see our chocolate recipe on page 28)

No trip to grandma's (nanna's we say in Australia) is complete without the customary biscuit tray, ready to be demolished by hungry kids. That is if daddy-o leaves any for the little ones.

Here's a healthy version of a choc chip biccy, so Nanna can still show love with food, but without killing dad.

How to make:

Preheat oven to 180°C.

In a large bowl, mix all inredients together.

Stir in the chocolate chunks.

Make small balls and press into cookie shape onto baking paper on a tray.

Bake at 130 degrees for 20 - 30 minutes.

Allow to cool for 10 minutes before removing from tray.

If you want your bikkies to look rougher (like anzac biscuits) just use shredded coconut as well as coconut flour.

Chocolate Crackle

Ingredients:

1 cup activated buckwheat

1 cup shredded coconut

4 tbsp of our chocolate spread (see our recipe on page 44)

Mixing rice crispies with chocolate has always been a party favourite, except that about 5 minutes later, the kids are uncontrollable...

Mitigate the madness with this delicious recipe, and keep your hair in your head!

How to make:

Mix all ingredients together in a bowl and spoon into cupcake papers.

Put in fridge for 30 minutes to allow to go hard.

Activating nuts and seeds:

Seeds are like potential, once you water them, they change state from seed to tiny plant. Activating seeds is just getting the seed to a point that it is about to shoot and then eating it.

To do so, just soak your seeds or nuts in water and keep rinsing until you see little shoots appear. Dry out in the sun or in the dehydrator.

Activated buckwheat tastes a million times better than unactivated. Try it for yourself...

Chocolate Milk

Ingredients:

1 cup coconut milk (or hemp milk or nut milk)

2 tbsp of cacao powder

1 fresh date (remove seed)

1 banana

1 cup of ice (optional)

Chocolate milk is a favourite with kids of all ages. Interestingly, the people who consume it the most are New Zealanders.

If you don't want to look like a New Zealander then drink up on this healthy alternative.

Just teasing our kiwi friends, you're beautiful.

How to make:

Blend all ingredients together and serve.

Chocolate Mousse

Ingredients:

4 fresh pitted dates

2 ripe avocados

1 ripe banana

1 tsp vanilla extract

⅓ cup raw cacao powder

Pinch of Himalayan sea salt

Chocolate Mousse is a favourite for fancy parties, where we try to act civilised.

Eat this chocolate mousse on it's own, or use it as icing on a cake, or just display your classiness by pouring it into a martini glass and floating a strawberry on top.

How to make:

Blend all the ingredients until smooth and creamy.

Add a splash of water or coconut water to make it a little fluffier.

Spoon into a bowl and allow to set in the fridge.

Chocolate Orange Bites

Kind of like a Jaffa, except not as sweet, and a little more classy. Oh, and it's super easy to make and tastes fantastic... Daahling.

Ingredients:

2 cups of shredded coconut

1 cup of freshly squeezed orange juice

¼ cup of coconut oil

1 tsp of orange rind

1 tsp of vanilla extract

2 tbsp of coconut nectar

¼ cup cacao powder

How to make:

Blend all ingredients together until creamy.

Spoon the mixture into chocolate moulds and freeze for about an hour.

Chocolate Spread

Chocolate spread, just like nutella, only without the nuts. A whole lot tastier and zero guilt. Enjoy eating this in front of your mum for breakfast!

1 cup of raw coconut oil

½ cup cacao powder

2 tbsp of coconut nectar

1 pinch of Himalayan sea salt

How to make:

Blend all ingredients together to form a paste.

Leave in the fridge for about 10 minutes if you like a thicker spread.

Can be added to slices of fruit like apple and also a great spread for our chocolate bread (page 30).

Coconut Rough

Ingredients:

Chocolate (see our recipe on page 28), before putting it into the fridge

1 cup shredded coconut

The cool thing about chocolate is that it can be used in so many different ways. An all time favourite is coconut rough. It is delicious and has a fun texture that we love.

How to make:

Mix the chocolate from the chocolate recipe on page 28 with the shredded coconut.

Pour into a shallow dish lined with baking paper and freeze for an hour.

Pull the slab out and cut or break it into pieces.

Cola

Ingredients:

1 tbsp maple syrup

1L soda water

OK, of all the recipes, this one is technically not sugar free. We ummed and aahed about putting it in, because maple syrup, although much better for you than sugar, is still a sugar.

But, and here comes the big but. For some people, a cola addiction is nearly impossible to kick, but unbelievably dangerous (even more so a diet cola addiction). So with this in mind, we have a cola substitute. But please, only use this to kick your cola addiction. First replace all the cola you drink with this, then cut down on the amount of maple syrup in your cola until you are left with plain old soda water.

How to make:

Mix a tablespoon of maple syrup into your bottle of soda water.

Every time you have it, reduce the amount of maple syrup until you don't need it anymore.

Crisps

2 beetroots or

2 bunches of kale, or

2 sweet potatoes

Himalayan sea salt

All spice mix

Crisps go hand in hand with a game on the TV. Until now, that hand in hand relationship has lead to an expanding waist line.

But no more!

You can still watch the game, and get some much needed nutrients into you.

How to make:

Preheat the oven to 180°C.

Slice the beetroot or sweet potato into wafer thin pieces (use a mandolin to do this easier).

If you're using Kale, separate the leaves from the stalks.

Put the chips onto a baking tray and bake for around 10 minutes or until crunchy.

Sprinkle salt or all spice over your chips and go enjoy the game!

Custard

Ingredients:

500ml coconut milk (or nut milk)

2 large eggs

2 tsp vanilla bean extract

1 tbsp tapioca flour

2 tbsp coconut nectar

Pinch of nutmeg

Ooh baby. Custard.

Amazing hot over freshly cooked cakes, or cold in a glass. Custard.

It even sounds delicious. Custard.

How to make:

Heat milk in a saucepan with vanilla and coconut nectar and bring to almost boiling point, then remove from the heat.

Beat the eggs and flour in a stainless steel mixing bowl until combined.

Pour the hot milk over the eggs and whisk in well.

Pour the whole mixture back into the saucepan and cook over a gentle heat, stirring until it thickens.

Remove from the heat and pour back into your large bowl.

Stir well until it cools down and smooths.

Serve hot or cold and enjoy.

Did you know?

To warm up a cold custard, place into a bowl and set it over a pan of simmering water. Stir and heat through gently.

Date and Banana Muffins

Date and banana muffins. Tasty tasty, but oh so hasty to come out the other end as a gust of wind.

Don't plan on being in any confined spaces after eating these. We'd also advise not to have these before a first date, otherwise you'll be dancing in your seat.

If you've been married for a while, then by all means eat double. You're going to be laughing so hard tonight as you wake your spouse up yelling "thunder storm!"

Ingredients:

3 ripe bananas

8 pitted dates, (2 dates sliced, set aside)

2 tsp cinnamon

½ cup coconut flour

1 tbsp baking powder

4 eggs

Pinch of Himalayan sea salt

How to make:

Preheat your oven to 180°C.

Mix all ingredients in a large bowl or blender until well combined.

Pour mixture into muffin cups or trays.

Add 1 thin slice of date to the top of each muffin.

Bake for 30 - 45 minutes.

Double Chocolate Cupcakes

All the girls from the gym are coming around for morning tea and you don't know what to put out?

You've got a birthday party and don't want to embarrass your kids by bringing out carrot sticks and celery?

Time to make some double chocolate cupcakes...

How to make the cupcake:

Preheat oven to 180°C.

Grease a mini cupcake tray with coconut oil.

Mix all ingredients together in a large bowl or blender.

Stir through the chocolate pieces.

Spoon the mixture into cupcake trays.

Bake for 20 - 30 minutes.

How to make the icing:

Stir all ingredients together.

Spread on your cake.

Cupcake Ingredients:

2 large eggs
¼ cup coconut oil
¼ cup coconut nectar
⅓ cup coconut flour OR ¾ almond meal
¼ cup cacao powder
1 tbsp baking powder
¼ cup water
½ cup HealthyJUNK chocolate, chopped

Icing Ingredients:

2 tbsp coconut nectar
2 tbsp raw cacao powder
1 tbsp coconut oil

Fish Fingers

Ingredients:

2 fish fillets, cut lengthways in half

¼ cup coconut flour

¼ cup unsweetened shredded coconut

⅛ tsp Himalayan sea salt

1 egg

2 tbsp coconut oil

Oh yum, fish fingers with fries (pg 64), tomato sauce (pg 120) and a bit of mayonnaise (pg 82). What could be a better choice for a lazy beach Sunday?

We don't know. But until we do, we'll just be eating these...

How to make:

Mix coconut flour, shredded coconut and sea salt together in a bowl.

Beat egg in separate bowl.

Dip fish fillet in egg, then roll in dry mixture.

Heat a frying pan over medium heat and add coconut oil when hot.

Pan-fry until fish is cooked through.

French Onion Dip

Ingredients:

1 onion (diced)

¼ tsp Himalayan sea salt

1 cup coconut oil

1 clove garlic, minced

1 cup sesame seed butter (see our recipe on page 100)

¼ tsp white pepper,

⅛ tsp cumin

¼ tsp celery salt

¼ cup homemade mayo (see our recipe on page 82)

1 ½ tbsp fresh parsley, chopped

1 tsp coconut aminos (tastes similar to soy sauce)

Dip goes well with chips. And until now, we have pretended it was healthy by putting carrot sticks onto the plate next to it.

The day after a party, there seems to be no dip, and no chips; but the carrot sticks are still there...

Now, you can combine the dip with the chips (page 50) and leave the carrots in the fridge and still have a shredded 6 pack.

How to make:

Sauté onions, garlic and sea salt in the coconut oil on low heat until it caramelises (about 20 minutes).

Add all the other ingredients into a food processor, then put one tablespoon of the sautéed onion in for flavour before blending it to a smooth texture.

Stir in the remaining caramelized onions for lumpy goodness.

Put the dip in the fridge. The longer you leave it, the nicer it tastes.

Fried Rice

Ingredients:

1 tbsp sesame oil

3 slices of bacon

1 medium cauliflower

1 onion diced

4 mushrooms sliced

2 eggs

1 tbsp grated ginger

2 tbsp of coconut oil

1 - 2 tbsp coconut aminos

1 tsp fish sauce

3 sliced shallots

Handful of coriander leaves

This is an amazing recipe. When you eat it, you feel like you are getting fatter and that your heart is going to explode from the overdose of high GI rice and refined fats of the cheap asian restaurant.

Until the next day. When you look better, feel better and your pants are looser.

Go on, make it - it will become your favourite dinner recipe, we promise. No rice, no bad fats and no guilt. BUT IT TASTES THE SAME!!!

Perfection in a pan.

How to make:

Slice bacon into strips and fry until crisp. Set aside.

Whisk eggs and fry like you would a thin omelette. Slice into strips and set aside.

Blend cauliflower in food processor until it looks like rice.

Fry onions in coconut oil until they are clear.

Add mushrooms, ginger and cauliflower. Stir fry until cooked through.

Stir in coconut aminos, sesame oil and fish sauce.

Put it all in a bowl with sliced egg, bacon strips, sliced green shallot and coriander leaves.

Tip over onto a plate to look fancy like the photo on the right.

Fries

Ingredients:

3 parsnips

1 tsp Himalayan sea salt

2 tbsp cold pressed olive oil

Would you like fries with that?

These actually taste exactly like fries you get from the big M. Except they are not going to clog your arteries. They are made of parsnips, not potatoes and they are delicious.

Especially if you combine them with a burger (page 22), cola (page 48) and tomato sauce (page 120).

Go on, do it. Make it an upsize...

How to make:

Cut parsnips into chip/French fry pieces using a Mandolin slicer.

Drizzle with oil.

Roast until tender and golden brown.

Sprinkle with sea salt and serve.

You could use sweet potato instead of parsnips, but they'll look like orange fries.

Ice Cream

Ingredients:

4 chopped frozen bananas

Dairy free, sugar free and deeeelicious!

Tastes just like any other icecream but without the aftertaste of guilt (and a swollen belly)

How to make:

Blend your bananas in a blender until smooth and creamy.

Different Flavours:

Strawberry - Add 1 cup of frozen strawberries.

Chocolate - 2 tablespoons of cacao powder.

Fruit and nut - ¼ cup of sultanas and roasted almonds.

Chewy caramel - 4 pitted dates chopped.
Put in freezer while you blend the bananas then stir the dates through.

Iced Coffee

Ingredients:

1 tsp of instant coffee or shot of espresso

1 cup of cold coconut milk (or hemp milk or nut milk)

1 cup of ice

Your morning pick me up doesn't have to be a cappuccino any more. Or a disgusting soy latte (along with the hormonal disruptions).

Just make yourself a delicious, healthy coffee shop alternative that tastes fantastic.

How to make:

Blend all ingredients together and serve in a cup.

NOTE: We have recipes of how to make your own dairy free milk in HealthyJUNK2.

Jaffa Balls

Jaffa Balls go great with a cup of coffee - they make you look sophisticated, like a 5 day cricket watcher. Or is that obsessive. Let's just have another Jaffa Ball and discuss it...

Ingredients:

2 cups of shredded coconut

1 cup of freshly squeezed orange juice

¼ cup of coconut oil

1 tsp of orange rind

1 tsp of vanilla extract

2 tbsp of coconut nectar

¼ cup cacao powder

4 dates (remove seeds)

How to make:

Blend all ingredients together well.

Roll into balls, 1cm in diameter.

Sprinkle some orange rind over the top to make it look fancy.
(You'll have most of an orange left.)

Lamingtons

Cake Ingredients:

3 eggs
¾ cup coconut flour
¼ cup Flax meal
1 tbsp baking powder
½ cup coconut oil
¼ cup coconut nectar
1 tsp vanilla extract
¾ cup water

Icing Ingredients:

½ cup cacao powder
½ cup coconut oil
2 tbsp coconut nectar
1 tsp vanilla extract
3 tbsp coconut milk
1 ½ cup shredded coconut

Lamingtons, the food of royalty.

How to make the sponge:

Preheat oven to 180°C (335°F).

Mix all ingredients together in a bowl.

Pour mixture into a greased pan.

Bake in oven for 20 minutes or until a toothpick inserted into the centre comes out clean.

Turn the sponge cake onto a wire rack to cool completely.

When the sponge cake has cooled down, cut into the size lamingtons you want.

How to make the icing:

Mix all ingredients (except shredded coconut) in a bowl.

Spread a thin layer of chocolate icing on all sides of each lamingtons.

Sprinkle shredded coconut on all sides before putting in the fridge to cool and set.

Lasagne

Mince Layer Ingredients:

2 onions, chopped
1 glove garlic
½ cup fresh basil
½ cup fresh oregano
2 carrots, grated or finely diced
10 mushrooms, finely diced
600g lean grass fed beef mince
1L (4 cups) tomato puree
4 diced tomatoes
2 – 3 generous tbsp no salt tomato paste
½ tsp smoked paprika
sea salt and pepper to taste

Pasta Layers:

1 large eggplant, sliced into 1 cm thin slices

Cauliflower Layers:

3 tbsp of olive oil
1 whole cauliflower
2 egg whites
1 tsp Himalayan sea salt
1 tbsp fresh basil
1 tbsp fresh parsley

How to make the Mince Layer:

Sauté the onion, garlic, carrot and mushrooms in a little olive oil over medium heat until softened.

Add the beef and cook for 5 – 10 minutes until browned.

Stir through the tomato paste and cook for about 3 minutes.
Add tomato and paprika.

Cover the pot and cook over a low heat for 30minutes until the sauce is thick and rich.

Season to taste and set the pot aside.

How to make the Cauliflower Layer:

Blend cauliflower and 2 egg whites together until it's a puree and then stir through fresh basil and parsley.

How to make the Eggplant Layer:

Pan fry eggplant pieces in a pan for 1 minute in olive oil with a sprinkle of salt and pepper before layering in Lasagne.

In a baking tray or lasagne dish, start layering the eggplant , then mince, then cauliflower sauce.

Keep layering until you fill baking dish, finishing with cauliflower sauce on top.

Cook in the oven at 180°C (355°F) for 40 minutes.

Garnish with fresh basil and a few cherry tomatoes.

Lemon Slice

Ingredients:

2 cups of shredded coconut

¼ cup of freshly squeezed lemon juice

¼ cup of coconut oil

1 tsp of grated lemon rind

1 tsp of vanilla extract

2 tbsp of coconut nectar

This is a recipe we've been using for years - it's a great way to get some good fats into your body, without making you fat!

Lemon slices are a fantastic little snack to keep in the fridge too, and just so easy to make.

How to make:

Blend all the ingredients together in a food processor until creamy.

Line a tray or dish with baking paper.

Press ingredients firmly into tray.

Place in freezer for about an hour before cutting into squares/shapes.

Lemonade

Ingredients:

Soda Water

Lemon

Honey (optional)

If you don't do cola, move onto lemonade and save yourself the high blood sugar issues!

It's so simple too...

How to make:

Squeeze a lemon into your glass of soda water.

If you're a sugar addict, you can put a tiny bit of honey in too, but remember that honey is a sugar, so you'll want to cut that back until you're just having lemon and water!

Mango Cupcakes

Cupcake Ingredients

4 eggs
1/3 cup coconut nectar
1/2 tbsp apple cider vinegar
1 tbsp vanilla extract
1/4 cup coconut or nut milk
1/3 cup coconut oil
1 cup of fresh mango purée
3/4 cup banana flour
1 tbsp baking powder
Pinch of Himalayan sea salt

Icing Ingredients

4 fresh pitted dates
1 ripe avocado
1 cup mango purée
1 tsp vanilla extract
1/3 cup raw cacao powder

How to make the cupcake:

Preheat the oven to 180°C.

Blend all ingredients together until smooth.

Pour the mixture into cupcake cups.

Put it in the oven for 30 minutes.

Let it cool completely before adding the icing.

How to make the icing:

Combine all the ingredients in a blender for 30 seconds until smooth and creamy.

Allow to set in fridge when you make the cupcakes.

Mayonnaise

Mayonnaise always makes us think about the movie Pulp Fiction, where they talk about how the French put mayonnaise on their fries, not ketchup.

If that's what you like, but you don't want to be a fatty, then here's the recipe for you!

Ingredients:

3 egg yolks at room temperature

1 tbsp lemon juice

1 tbsp regular natural mustard

Pinch of Himalayan sea salt

Pinch of pepper

250g grape seed oil

How to make:

Put egg yolks into blender or bowl and whisk/blend until smooth.

Add lemon juice, mustard and salt and pepper and blend until mixed.

Very slowly drizzle oil while blending or whisking at low speed.

Store in fridge up to 1 week.

Muesli

Ingredients:

1 cup coconut flakes

1 cup activated buckwheat

1 cup sunflower seeds

1 cup pepitas

½ cup sesame seeds

½ cup goji berries

3 tbsp of chia seeds

2 tbsp of coconut oil

2 tbsp of coconut nectar

Any other dried fruit, seed or nut that you desire

Health food manufacturers have caught onto the idea that muesli is better for you than cereal.

The problem they have is that muesli tastes so much better (and makes them so much more money) when it is laced with sugar.

Here's a recipe that will have you feeling full until lunch time, but tastes fantastic.

How to make:

Preheat oven to 180°C.

Mix all ingredients together.

Lay baking paper in tray.

Spread the mixture out over the tray.

Bake in oven for 15 minutes until golden brown and crispy.

*Because of Julius' nut allergy we have no nuts, but if you eat nuts, you can add some raw unsalted almonds or cashews to this recipe if you like.

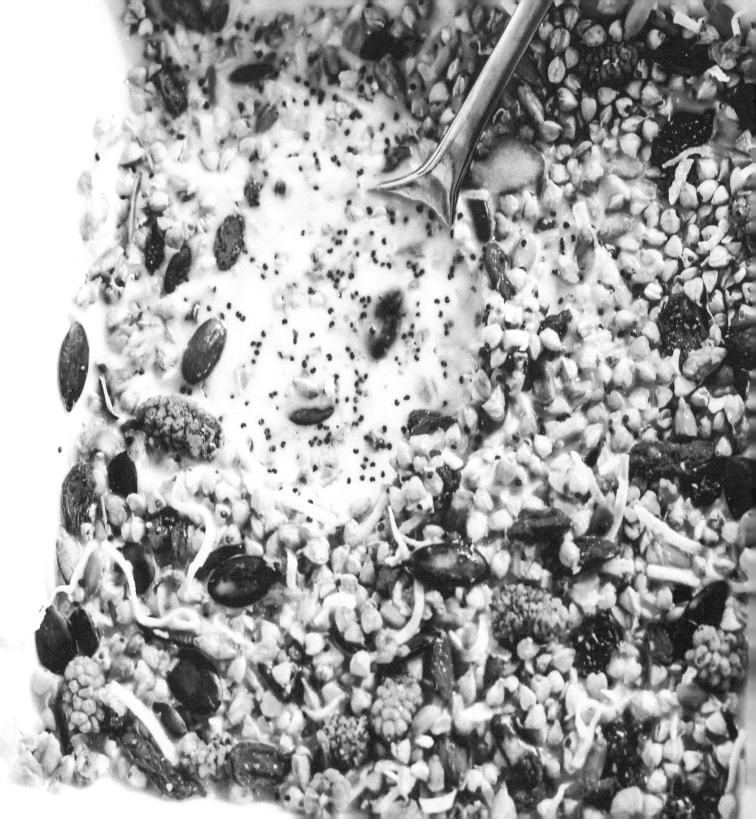

Muesli Bar

Want to clear out your system really fart?

(that was on purpose).

Ingredients:

10 large medjool dates, seeds removed

½ cup coconut oil

¼ cup cacao powder

1 cup pumpkin seeds

1 cup dried shredded coconut

4 tbsp chia seeds soaked in ¼ cup of water

1 cup sunflower seeds

½ cup sesame seeds

½ cup goji berries

2 tbsp poppy seeds

How to make:

Blend all ingredients until well combined.

Spread the batter evenly into a baking dish that is lined with baking paper and press down firmly.

Place in the fridge or freezer for about 30 minutes before cutting into bars.

Nuggets

Ingredients:

2 boneless, skinless chicken breasts cut into cubes

¼ cup coconut flour

¼ cup unsweetened shredded coconut

⅛ tsp Himalayan sea salt

1 egg

2 tbsp coconut oil

Chicken nuggets, every kids favourite in their happy meals. Now you can make them at home and they don't need to be limited to 6 - give them as many as they want because they are healthy!

How to make:

Mix coconut flour, shredded coconut and sea salt together in a bowl.

Beat egg in separate bowl.

Dip chicken cube in egg, then roll in dry mixture.

Heat a frying pan over medium heat and add coconut oil when hot.

Pan-fry until chicken is cooked through.

Serve with tomato sauce (page 120).

Onion Rings

If you're not into fries, we'll bet your choice is onion rings. Here's a recipe that makes onion rings as tasty as their deep fried artery blocking cousins, but without the health risks.

Ingredients:

2 medium onions

¾ cup banana flour (or gluten-free flour of choice)

3 large eggs

1 tbsp all purpose seasoning

How to make:

Preheat oven to 180°C.

Slice the onions and separate into rings.

Place them in a bowl of water.

Mix flour and seasoning together in a bowl.

Beat eggs in a separate bowl.

Dip wet onion ring in dry mixture, then egg, then roll in dry mixture again.

Place them on a baking tray and bake for about 10 minutes before turning each ring (or you can just stir them).

Continue baking until brown and very crispy on both sides.

Pad Thai

Cooked ingredients:
1 package Konjac fettuccine (basically a fibre that tastes like noodles)
½ cup raw sunflower seeds
200g boneless, skinless chicken breasts cut into cubes
4 eggs, whisked
2 medium sized shallots, finely chopped
5 cloves of garlic, chopped
¾ cup chopped onion
1 cup Mung beans
3 carrots, julienned
½ cup fresh coriander
1 lime, quartered
Himalayan sea salt
Ground black pepper

Sauce Ingredients:
2 tbsp lime juice
5 tbsp fish sauce
5 tbsp coconut aminos
2 tbsp apple cider vinegar
3 tbsp coconut nectar
¾ tsp ground ginger
½ tsp pepper
diced chilli (optional)

Because of Julius' nut allergy, we have always had to avoid this dish (sad, we know). One day we met the lady who owns our local Thai restaurant and she swore that she would cook Julius his first Pad Thai (ooh the excitement) without nuts.

He fell in love with it, just like anyone else who tries Thai.

How to make:

Pulse the sunflower seeds in a blender to break them up.

Pan-fry them in coconut oil or olive oil until they smell delicious and set aside.

Fry the chicken pieces with the onions, set aside.

Scramble the eggs in the frying pan and pour into the same bowl as the chicken.

Stir fry all the remaining ingredients really fast (they should still be a bit crunchy).

Prepare the fettuccine as described on the packet.

Combine the dressing ingredients in a glass jar with lid and shake.

Combine all the cooked ingredients in a large bowl and toss.

Pour dressing over and toss again.

To make it look fancy, put it into noodle boxes that you can buy from a $2 shop.

Paddle Pop

Ingredients:

4 large ripe bananas, peeled and cut in half

Chocolate (see our recipe on page 28)

¼ cup shredded coconut

Paddle pops are a summer favourite. Who can forget the chocolate dripping down your arm as you battle the brain freeze from the icecream.

That was before we got fat. Since then, we have had to stay away from paddle pops. But no more!

Get yours made today...

How to make:

Line a baking sheet with baking paper.

Insert a Popsicle stick into the base of each piece of banana.

Put melted chocolate into glass jar so you can dip banana.

Dip each banana in the melted chocolate.

Sprinkle it with coconut.

Place the bananas on the baking sheet and freeze for 2 hours.

Pancakes

Ingredients:

4 eggs

2 bananas

1 tbsp coconut oil

2 tbsp coconut flour (optional)

1 tsp of cinnamon

This book wouldn't be complete without the customary pancake. It's what you have for breakfast when nobody is looking - when you are put up in a hotel for work and you have a few hours to kill at the buffet breakfast...

Now you can eat them at home, with friends! Give them to your kids, with icecream (page 66)... for breakfast!

How to make:

Mix eggs, bananas and cinnamon together in a blender.

Add the mixture to a hot pan of coconut oil.

Top it with whatever you like!

Pasta

3 or 4 Large Zucchini

Before anyone told us that wheat is why we are fat, we all knew it. Pasta, the staple dish of Italy is just not good to the Western man or woman's stomach.

But don't worry, you can make pasta out of zucchini, just spiral it in a machine like the one below, soak it in boiling water for a few minutes and you won't be able to tell the difference (we tried it on our teenage son and his friends and they couldn't tell the difference).

You can peel the zucchini first so they don't ask what the green is in the pasta!

Peanut Butter

Ingredients:

3 cups sunflower seeds

Peanut free peanut butter. It tastes exactly the same as peanut butter, but won't kill the peanut allergy kid in the family.

Well, it's not really the taste that is so appealing about peanut butter - it's the texture. This recipe will make a jar of peanut butter that you will swear is peanut butter - except for the anaphylaxis.

How to make:

Preheat oven to 180°C degrees.

Spread sunflower seeds on baking tray.

Roast in oven for 10 minutes until slightly brown.

Allow to cool.

Blend in high-speed blender until smooth.

Crunchy:

For crunchy, set aside a half-cup of the roasted sunflower seeds and stir through the blended seeds at the end.

Pour into a glass jar.

Store in fridge (if it gets there).

NOTE: You may need to add a little oil.

Pesto

Ingredients:

1 large bunch parsley

1 large bunch basil

1 clove garlic

½ cup of roasted sunflower seeds

2 tbsp lime juice

Pinch of black pepper

Pinch of Himalayan sea salt

4 tbsp flaxseed oil

Pesto is delicious. It's not actually junk food, but it is made with pine nuts normally. Here is a recipe that will help out our poor nut allergy sufferers to experience the culinary delight that is... pesto.

How to make:

Blend all the ingredients to a fine paste.

Keep in the fridge for up to a week.

Pizza

You honestly won't notice any difference between a gourmet bought pizza and one you make at home with a cauliflower crust. It is delicious and our favourite recipe.

We haven't given a recipe for the topping, because everyone has a different favourite, so have fun making yours!

Enjoy!

Ingredients for base:

1 small head cauliflower
1 egg
1 tsp Himalayan sea salt
1 tbsp fresh chopped basil
1 tbsp fresh chopped parsley
½ tsp of garlic (optional)

Ingredients for topping:

1 cup tomato paste, then anything you love!

How to make:

Preheat oven to 180°C.

Chop your cauliflower up and light cook it until just soft.

Blend cauliflower and the squeeze liquid out in a kitchen towel/cloth.

Mix the other ingredients with the cauliflower.

Line a pizza tray with baking paper and your pizza mix.

Cook for 15 - 20 minutes.

Spread on 100% tomato paste with a knife and top with your favourite ingredients before baking in the oven at 180°C for another 30 minutes.

NOTE: We opt for no cheese (you really don't notice the difference except that you don't have the heavy feeling).

Quiche

These 'egg pies' are a staple in our house. They are a perfect portion sized breakfast that can be packed into a lunch box for a filling, nutritious snack.

Ingredients:

12 pieces of rindless bacon

12 eggs

Handful of fresh garlic chives finely sliced

Inch slice white goats milk cheese (crumbled)

Diced fresh tomato

Avocado (cut into cubes)

How to make:

Preheat oven on 200°C.

Slice bacon lengthways in half and line the outside of each muffin cup with bacon halves.

Add eggs and all other ingredients to mixing bowl and beat with fork. Pour into each muffin cup of muffin tray.

Feel free to add other ingredients like mushrooms, beans, zucchini etc.

Bake in oven for about 15 minutes.

Allow 10 minutes to cool.

Can be eaten warm or cold as a snack and kids LOVE them in their lunch boxes.

Red Velvet Cupcakes

Cupcake Ingredients:

1/2 cup beetroot juice (1 whole beetroot peeled, blended and juice squeeze out for juice)
4 eggs
½ cup coconut oil
½ cup coconut nectar
1 tbsp vanilla extract
1 tsp baking powder (see our recipe)
1 pinch Himalayan sea salt
½ cup banana flour

Icing ingredients:

¾ cup raw cashews, soaked 3 hours and rinsed
2 tbsp coconut oil, melted
3 tbsp coconut nectar
1 tsp vanilla essence
1 tsp fresh lemon juice
¼ tsp sea salt

These new bad boys to the junk food party are to die for daahling. Now you don't actually have to die of a heart attack when you eat them. Holy sheet they are delicious!

How to make cupcakes:

Preheat oven to 180°C.

Blend all cupcake ingredients together well.

Pour into greased cupcake cups.

Bake for 30 - 40 minutes, or until an inserted toothpick comes out clean.

Cool completely before icing.

How to make the icing:

Blend the icing ingredients until creamy in a high speed blender.

Put in bowl and leave in fridge for at least 1 hour to thick.

If you have time, keep it in fridge overnight (so do these the day before).

NOTE: If you have a nut allergy like Julius, use the chocolate spread as the icing! It's delicious!

Rice

Ingredients:

Cauliflower

Rice, like pasta and mashed potato, has become a staple in most people's diets. The problem with each of these is that they are packed with high GI carbs - the stuff that makes you eat more than you should and become fat.

We make rice with a cauliflower - and you can't even tell the difference (but your waist line will!)

How to make:

Blend cauliflower in food processor until it resembles rice (just a few seconds).

Cook in a pot of already boiling water (just like rice except it only takes about 3 minutes).

Strain and serve.

NOTE: If you want more flavour in your rice, add whatever garlic, herbs and spices you like!

Scones

Ingredients:

¼ cup coconut flour

¼ cup banana flour

1 tsp baking powder

¼ cup coconut nectar or honey (optional for sweetness)

¼ cup coconut oil

½ cup coconut milk (or nut milk)

3 eggs

We've never made real scones before, but we've certainly eaten them. Usually when we're travelling; they seem to be a staple for the breakfast buffet at most hotels.

Here is a simple recipe to make your own scones, without any junk in them!

How to make:

Preheat oven to 180°C.

Mix all ingredients together.

Put mixture into cupcake boxes.

Bake in 180°C (350°F) oven for 30 minutes until golden brown.

Cool on a wire rack before peeling off the cupcake box.

These are delicious with some of our 'Peanut' butter (page 100) or Jam recipe (see HealthyJUNK2).

Spaghetti Bolognese

Ingredients:

2 onions, chopped

2 carrots, finely diced

10 mushrooms, finely diced

1 glove garlic

500g lean grass fed beef mince

2 – 3 generous tbsp no-salt tomato paste

4 diced tomatoes

½ teaspoon smoked paprika

½ cup fresh basil

½ cup fresh oregano

Friday carb load before the big game.

Except that we overeat and the big game becomes the big lame. "I got a stitch," or that really *heavy in the guts* feeling are a thing of the past with our delicious, light spag-bol recipe that tastes exactly like the real thing!

How to make:

Sauté the onion, garlic, carrot and mushrooms in a little olive oil over medium heat until softened.

Add the beef and cook for 5 – 10 minutes until brown.

Stir through the tomato paste and cook for about 3 more minutes.

Add tomato and paprika.

Cover the pot and bubble over a low heat for 30 minutes until the sauce is thick and rich.

For the last 10 minutes, throw in the basil and oregano.

Serve over our zucchini pasta (page 98).

Spring Roll

Ingredients:

Cabbage Leaves

Carrot

Red Capsicum

Meat of your choice
(pork, chicken or prawn work
well)

Diced Onion

Coconut Aminos

Mushrooms

Nothing says "I'm fancy, sophisticated and worldly" like eating spring rolls with a pair of chopsticks. Until you drop one on your lap.

Get that authentic "worldly" look with the Iron Chef appeal by making these unbelievably healthy versions of our favourite asian dish...

How to make:

Slice your meat into strips.

Slice your veggies into strips (except the cabbage).

Pre-cook the meat and diced onions in a small amount of coconut aminos to give it that Asian taste.

Throw the mushrooms in for the last couple of minutes (otherwise they just disintegrate).

Roll all of your ingredients into a cabbage leaf.

Steam in your vegetable steamer for about 10 minutes.

If you want to look fancy, buy some of those bamboo steamer dishes for your steaming.

Serve with sauce of your choice, we love sweet chilli sauce with these.

Sweet Chilli Sauce

Sweet chilli sauce is normally made with a ton of sugar (it's why it is so morish!)

Make this delicious sweet chilli recipe yourself in about 5 minutes, (it has no sugar.)

Ingredients:

1 long red chilli

1 red capsicum

1 clove garlic

A tiny little piece of ginger

4 fresh pitted dates

1 lime

Pinch of Himalayan sea salt

Pinch of black pepper

How to make:

Seed the chilli and the capsicum.

Gather the seeds and put into a bowl.

Put chilli, capsicum, garlic, dates, lime, sea salt and pepper into blender for 30 seconds.

Mix the seeds in for the last second or two to give that sweet chilli look.

If you want bite, mix in the chilli seeds, if not, then just the capsicum seeds.

Put into a glass jar and store it in the fridge for 2 weeks.

Tomato Sauce

Ingredients:

1 tsp olive oil

1 garlic cloves

1 onion

2 tbsp apple cider vinegar

2 tbsp red wine vinegar

2 tbsp coconut nectar

$\frac{1}{2}$ tsp Himalayan sea salt

400g can tomato puree

170g tomato paste (no salt)

$\frac{1}{4}$ tsp ground cloves

$\frac{1}{4}$ tsp oregano

Tomato Sauce, it's good on just about anything.

Make your own, and avoid all the hidden nasties of the bought stuff.

How to make:

Heat oil and sauté garlic until fragrant.

Add onion and cook until softened.

Pour in vinegars, coconut nectar and salt.

Bring to boil before adding tomato puree and paste.

Bring to boil again before adding cloves and oregano.

Simmer for 20 minutes until sauce thickens.

Blend until smooth.

Store on a glass jar in fridge for up to 2 weeks.

Top Deck Loaf

Ingredients:

½ cup coconut flour

½ cup banana flour

1 tbsp baking powder

1 pinch of Himalayan sea salt

¼ cup cacao powder

¼ cup coconut oil

3 large eggs, room temperature

¾ cup of water

½ cup coconut nectar

Add 1 avocado to the mix if you want moist bread. (optional)

Every attempt at making white chocolate to taste like white chocolate has failed. When we get it right, we'll make another cookbook, but until then, try the top deck loaf. It has the consistency of bread (not the lightness of a cake).

But it is delicious and looks quite sophisticated...

How to make:

Preheat oven to 180°C.

Mix all ingredients together (except cacao powder).

Divide the batter in half.

Add the cacao powder to one half to make the chocolate base.

Pour chocolate half into the bottom of greased loaf pan.

Spoon the remaining batter on top and bake until an inserted toothpick comes out clean.

Vegetable Stack

Ingredients:

12 eggs

1 head broccoli

200g pumpkin

1 red capsicum

1 yellow capsicum

2 - 3 zucchini

200g sweet potato

8 mushrooms

2 carrots

¼ cup Pesto (see our recipe on page102)

This freezes well and is great for work lunches along with the quiche (see our recipe on page 106)

How to make:

Preheat your oven to 180°C.

Slice the all veggies into pieces about 1cm thick (it doesn't matter if some pieces are a bit bigger or smaller).

Grate the carrots.

Whisk the eggs together with the pesto then mix in the grated carrots.

Layer all veggies in a baking dish.

Pour the egg mixture over the top (it will soak through).

Bake for about 45 minutes or until cooked.

Slice and serve.

Wedges

Ingredients:

4 medium sweet potatoes

2 tbsp all purpose seasoning

2 tbsp cold pressed olive oil

Some tomato sauce (see our recipe on page 120)

Some mayonnaise (see our recipe on page 82)

Wedges are what pubs make because they want to charge more than they could with fries.

We love wedges, especially with sour cream and tomato sauce (page 120) or sweet chilli sauce (page 118).

For the sour cream, use mayonnaise (page 82) or you could use Greek yoghurt (not dairy free, but it is a darn side better for you than sour cream - and it tastes the same when put with wedges).

How to make:

Mix oil and spices in a baking tray.

Cut potatoes into wedges and coat with oil mix using your hands.

Roast until tender and golden brown.

Sprinkle with sea salt and serve.

White Christmas

Ingredients:

³/₄ cup sunflower seeds

¹/₂ cup coconut concentrate

¹/₄ cup coconut flakes

4 medjool dates (remove seeds)

1 tbsp coconut oil, melted

1 tsp vanilla extract

Pinch of Himalayan sea salt

¹/₂ cup strawberries

You no longer have a good excuse to be a dump truck over the christmas holiday. Make up this recipe and everyone will love you for it, because they won't have to make a weight loss new year's resolution!

How to make:

Blend all ingredients except strawberries, in a food processor.

Pulse in strawberries until they are broken down and well mixed in.

Transfer mixture into a small bread pan and press down into bottom evenly.

Set in freezer for about 30 minutes.

Remove from freezer and cut into pieces.

Store in the fridge if you have any left over.

Talk to us!

We'd love to hear from you, please let us know if and how this book has helped you; or tell us your family's story of going from junk food family to healthy family. Just shoot us a quick email at

sharnyandjulius@sharnyandjulius.com

Thankyou for taking the time to read our book!

Sharny and Julius Kieser

You can also follow us on social media by searching:
sharnyandjulius
The Kiesers

CPSIA information can be obtained
at www.ICGtesting.com
Printed in the USA
LVHW070845050519
616679LV00005B/10/P